I0438526

The 5 Food Groups

Negotiating In Relationships

Relationship and internet dating help for everyone who
wants a better cleaner faster relationship

One hour of your
time reading
this book will
enlighten you

By M. Lyman Hill

author of My First 32 Coffee Dates

The 5 Food Groups
Negotiating in Relationships

By M. Lyman Hill

**Relationship and Internet dating help for anyone who
wants a better cleaner faster relationship**

Copy Editing by: Valerie Peck

LEGAL NOTICE
Author: M. Lyman Hill
Title: The 5 Food Groups

Copyright © 2011, M. Lyman Hill
Round-2 Communications Presents

ALL RIGHTS RESERVED. This book contains material protected under International and Federal Copyright Laws and Treaties. Any unauthorized reprint or use of this material is prohibited. No part of this book may be reproduced or transmitted in any form or by any means, electronic or mechanical, including photocopying, recording, or by any information storage and retrieval system without express written permission from the author.

*W*ake-up call

Hey, someone has to manage finances, household chores, life direction, free time and sex; whether it is both of you or one of you; life needs at least a little management or things fall apart. There is a law which applies to all things in life: "if you don't put energy into a thing, the thing tends to decay" – this is called the law of entropy and decay is how we can describe relationships that people don't put energy into. Energy does not mean "work, effort, drama", it means power as in "empowered" relationship members.

There is a segment of people who believe that things will just work out but thing don't tend to work out unless at least a little wisdom and energy is put into them.

This book helps you energize your relationship processes and redefine and streamline decision making as a couple. If you adopt the 5 food groups you can solve almost any obstacle to fulfillment and harmony. The two areas the 5 food groups cannot solve are apathy and ignorance.

This book provides a path to greater connection, intimacy and better communication through good relationship management.

*I*ntroductions

The divorce rate is declining a little and the rate at which couples are marrying is also declining; showing that men and women are adapting to the reasons people couple up and get divorces. Since 1970 the number of men and women living together in increased 10 fold.

There is also strong evidence that the more education and prepared a couple gets the greater longevity they will enjoy. The prepared educated couple stays together about 86% of the time. There is also a ray of hope in that the divorce rate of couple's declines with age. Presuming that we get smarter with age, stop getting married, or find reasons to ignore what would have caused a divorce when we were younger.

The funny thing is these trends and statistics don't really tell the "quality" and "fulfillment" story. Are couples any better off emotionally or physically now that we have chosen not to marry or does that just mean splitting up is simpler? Perhaps by not marring we are saying we see the possibility of splitting up and want an easier path to that when it happens?

So the discussion of what one can negotiate in long-term relationships changes from just staying together to what can be negotiated for a better quality of relationship for both mates. Relationships have gotten more complex; as destiny and arranged relationships have been replaced by smarter men and women looking for each other in the information age.

Modern relationship has become more temporary and as a response many of us are questioning why? Many are taking action to see how to make relationship better for themselves and their mate.

Why would anyone want to continuously try the same old things when test after test has shown it will fail? This is how we as people have been approaching relationship. We somehow see relationships modeled to us, attempt it and then see it has issues. The relationship then goes kaput.

There are just something's about relationships that are easy to fix and the 5 food groups are those things. They reduce strife, streamline decision making and set the stage for negotiations and fulfillment. *A Better Relationship Foundation….*

I spent a great deal of time after my divorce thinking about what it was that I did wrong. That woman called me a "monster", me who is one of the nicest guys in the world. I was 38 years old and broken, searching for answers.

It took years of counseling and friendly conversations to conclude that anyone can be a monster to someone they are not compatible with and the best relationships are built when "being ourselves" is a benefit to our mates. Being me hurt my ex and there was not a thing I could do about it because I cannot change my core person. This also gave me the definition of a soul mate "when we being ourselves are a benefit to our mates and they being themselves are a benefit to us in return". Essentially a relationship with a soul mate is a relationship you don't have to work at. And better yet, if you choose to work at it you can find the kind of fulfillment you always dreamed of.

After the millennium I began to research what makes couples happy and to my surprise I could not find many couples who were all that happy. Their marriages had survived but happiness has eluded them. What I mean by happy is fulfilled. In large part couple grew more complacent and distant over time and though some stayed together is was not inspiring. I could sense it in their answers, they were in love and committed but the fire was just not there.

I did meet some couples who seemed happy enough and they had a little advice for me which I noted and then thought "the test of time with prove them right or wrong".

I began to wonder if relationships in this day and age were meant to be temporary. I wondered given the rate of divorce and my own experience, if temporary relationships were the new "reality" we all faced.

I questioned "coupling up" and "tradition" as both being something people have done for time in memorial which had not changed much even though we seemed to have new rules of engagement and laws of attraction.

In 2004 I began a relentless drive to connect to a soul mate and to understand, "like an engineer understands", what it takes to locate her. The 5 food groups came out of these experiences and I think you'll find them helpful both in helping you find the right mate and in building a better relationship. People already coupled up can use them to forge a better relationship.

I used the food groups to ask more refined questions to women. The food groups helped me quickly see how compatible I would be in a relationship with them in the way we make decisions and conduct ourselves. The 5 food groups go beyond personality and compatibility testing to real life situational examples with cognitive reasoning.

The food groups were a great way to explore more designer relationships where a woman and I can design a nice workable arrangement customized for us. The food groups opened my eyes to a brave new world. There are thing we can successfully do in relationships to make relationships better, in this day and age we can customize a relationship to make it fit both partners given their willingness to participate in negotiations.

The 5 food groups are those elements we can and often do successfully negotiate in relationships that are a win for everyone.

What are the 5 food groups?

The 5 food groups are "things" we do after we couple up. All couple do these things in theory and getting good at them is a benefit to both mates and the relationship.

There are 5 areas of relationships couples can and often do successfully negotiate. There are lots of other things besides these 5 areas you may be able to negotiate but these 5 are the most successful because they are not interfering with our core person.

Finances

Financial control has long been the domain of men; it is ultimate control of a relationship. In times past financial control was a kin to blackmail for men to get what they wanted and to keep women inline and in the marriage. When a woman had no control, she found it difficult to impossible to invoke change, take care of herself, or leave.

The traditional model still exists today and there is a newer model that immerged in the 1970 when couples started living together where one mate would "handle" finances such as paying the bills or the couple would separate their finances unless there was an advantage to joining them; such as to qualify for a mortgage loan.

Free Time

Time doing what you want comes after the decision to "make time" for others, time together, time apart, time for our common interests, time with friends, time with hobbies -- all take away from our free time. Free time includes decisions we make for our time that take an effort -- will he put the toilet seat down or clean up his socks; will she? It takes time to take the garbage out. His choices affect you, if you feel you must do something because he did not.

Household Chores

If you have a maid, a gardener and a handy man then this just got easier but if not there is a lot of work to keeping a house going. There is laundry, shopping for food and sundries, taking the trash out. If you control free time you likely also control chores because they can be added to a schedule and you can train someone to do it as you would. Management 101 - delegation of responsibility.

Household chores have long been the domain of women and children in traditional relationships which spilled over into the mind set of those in modern relationships. In our surveys women indicated even if he was willing to do all the chores she still wanted to own most of them and get his help when she wanted. Tradition remains pervasive.

Life Direction

A decision to move, improve one's education, have children, take on renting borders, make or leave friendships. Of course this takes time so one can control it with free time such as spend your free time in class improving our education. There is also the personal/spiritual/cultural/sexual direction of a person's life. Many couples have wrestled with a move for his career.

Sex

We all want spontaneous sex but most of us have it at night in our bedrooms and it is likely something you have done before. Control of sex can mean saying yes or no, what and when, how, who, how much or how hard. Sex takes time too, so controlling time is key to controlling sex.

Sex is another element of relationships that has been used as a weapon. Men and women too often think of sex as an entitlement. Partners sometimes provide sexual benefit to each other for reasons other than pleasure.

- To stop him from straying
- It is my duty
- To have children

Women are known to have medium to low libido compared to men as a group. It is also common knowledge that sex gets a little less exciting and intense after a relationship has gone on for a time.

This food group is likely the most flexible as it is most often done in private with discretion and between two committed people.

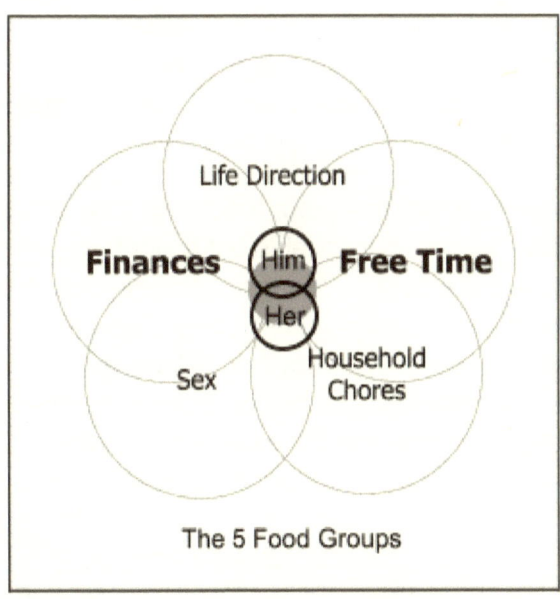

The 5 Food Groups

The 5 food groups are things and spheres of influence. The amount of control you allow in your relationship changes the overlap at the center which is your relationship. Most people give a little control so the union of a food group and your relationship is relatively small. An example might be the amount of sexual choices a woman might allow control over – most women will not do every kind of sex act or give up control over their choice to keep a pregnancy or terminate it.

Limitations

People in relationships are not all that connected. Members of relationships even long-term ones most often don't mingle everything. Women and men maintain control of their bodies, health choices; reserve the right to say no, and won't breach ethical or moral boundaries, maintain separate savings and retirement accounts. Even in committed relationships people reserve decisions to themselves so their ability to influence their mate is limited by how much control they allow their mate.

When we are young (in our teens and 20s) and get together we are more pliable but as time passes we become more baked. Young people are looking for answers while more mature people often have reasons for believing what they believe and, they have a life already with assets. Trust is the main enabler of control. If a mate has a million dollar retirement going into a relationship it will take some trust to allow any control over that money. In modern relationships people often make prenuptial agreements and even couple just living together have legal agreements.

Those boundaries a mate is <u>not</u> <u>willing</u> <u>to</u> <u>negotiate</u> are '*Hard*' boundaries. Hard boundaries may be pushed over time or as trust grows. Some couples even ask for this so they can get past trust issues. Pushing hard boundaries is stressful and can cause strife.

The areas a mate is willing to negotiate are called 'Pliable' boundaries. A mate likely has a level of comfort they are willing to allow and then they have a grey area of unknown comfort where statements like "I have not tried that" or "I am willing to give it a try but I never even heard of that" come into the conversation.

Must haves and deal breakers

Creating a list of must haves is the same as setting boundaries; some people also call a special set of boundaries "deal breakers." When you examine the attributes you want in a partner (and don't want) and what you want from life and relationship -- the must haves are a guide to get what and who you are looking for. In existing relationship they are a guide to how far you need to go to reach fulfillment. Must haves are your guide to personal fulfillment.

If your 'must have' list consists of simply the physical like: Tall, Blond, Great Body, Nice Smile and Rich then the weighted matters of life, that get people the most fulfillment, are unrecognized as are the boundaries of your decision making.

The deal breakers I created were: 1) No STD's, 2) I have kids and an extended family which I am not willing to exclude. My must haves started with "Companionship" being most important to me in a relationship above all other things, followed by "communication", then a "strong intimate connection". Your desire for control can be a must have.

Important like to haves

Your 'like to have' list will consist of those things you want to aspire to as well as attributes you like to have now but are willing to wait for. My list included the activities I most cherished and want to share and a set of common values and political views. This list might include the thing in your current or past relationship you most wanted but did without.

Avoid pent up desires as 'must haves'

One woman I talked to who had just come out of a bad relationship insisting she get the things she was denied in the past relationship. I explained to her the desire to attain something just because it is amplified by your disappointment or sense of loss does not elevate it to must have status. Yes you want it but elevating it because you did not experience it before should be a warning "you really don't know how your experience will fare."

This is how transitional and healing relationships go wrong, when a mate places strong emphasis on the things they did not get in past relationships and when they happen they discover they were not as important as originally felt. This kind of insistence is a kin to a midlife crisis where decisions to buy wheeled vehicles that are red and convertible because the level of fulfillment in a relationship did not allow the mate to satisfy whatever need they had; was not fulfilling.

*E*qual or not equal that is the question?

Why do I need to know this?

The reality of relationships is they are not equal and cannot be without some re-socialization by both mates. It helps to visualize where your relationship is to see how far you want to go to make it "best".

The 50/50 relationship

No one knows for sure but sometime in the 1960-70 and likely out of feminism sprang a new relationship model for men and women: the 50/50 relationship.

50/50 seems to be the unspoken ideal right now among urban and professional couples. The ideal goes that the partners in the relationship will natural assume responsibilities and roles they are good at but at all times remain equal and make at least critical decisions together. No one is leading and no one is following; essentially a democracy.

However there is another new norm where men and women don't think of themselves as equals. In the past it was assumed that men were more capable leaders, but that is not the case anymore. Yet men believe things about themselves that may or may not be true they tend to rate women as weaker and less capable. Women on the other hand, believe things about themselves that may or may not be true and rate men as inferior in many areas. People in general see themselves in a better light then they actually are comparatively to others in their gender and the other gender.

The dynamic has changed because women are more educated and independent. The beliefs people hold color our view of our partner's abilities and change our comfort level of trust in them. Here is an example: a woman as the main protector of the family when the man out weighs her by 80 pounds and she is 5' 2" tall and shy. She could buy a gun, take karate classes. My grandmother could have fit this role but who would naturally see her that way?

Then what we believe about ourselves also limits us. Like the woman who wants the man to help with household chores then feels the need to correct everything he is doing because it does not meet her standard. So instead of teaching him how and helping him develop skills that meet her standards she limits herself to the role of de facto housekeeper and discourages him. So the guy is big and harry with a beard, who would see him naturally as a housekeeper or home maker?

We must admit making decisions about dinner and returning to college have a different weight. Let's say a partner in a 50/50 relationship wants to return to collage so the couple has a powwow. One partner thoughtfully says no and the other yes. That is a stalemate. Of course the partner wishing to go to college could act independently and return to school against the wishes of the other partner but that does not take into account "the couple".

The 50/50 relationship ideal is not all that equal and it is so new that who knows if it will survive. I suppose there have been 50/50 relationships in theory forever, but in practice they are not all that equal because of our cultural stereotyping.

With decision making you can see strength and weakness in the 50/50 relationship right off. The strength is two minds might make a better decision and the weakness is two minds might not make better decisions and might not ever agree.

The problem inherent in 50/50 relationships with unspoken, unmet or unrealized expectations and two people who are not the best at communicating is the wedge that occurs with unmet expectations. The obvious solution to the problem is getting better at communication and telling your known expectations.

Then again imagine the gridlock of two minds disagreeing and no tie breaker. So decision making may or may not be easy depending on the people and their communication skills.

The traditional relationship

Consider for a moment the traditional western relationship that is somewhat to completely male dominated. The relationship either came out of western culture, or religion or both or survives today as the default model for couples who don't have other dreams. We see it modeled all the time but no one learns about it in school. It is implicit in the terms husband and wife. Yes the husband is different from the wife, they are not quite partners. He should be the primary bread winner and she the primary caregiver and a family should ensue.

If we look at the Christian version we see the wife "obeying" and "submitting" to the husband; now that sounds very equal. Even in the secular model there is a stark difference between male and female roles with the man as protector, governor and primary provider and the women as a support to him and the family.

Decisions in these types of relationships might be elegantly made by the leader or "he can make them when she lets him". There are obvious avenues for abuse of breach of trust and obvious avenues for a perfect union. Once again depends on how well the couple communicates and how well their roles are defined.

The transitional (healing) relationship

After you break up with someone there are sometimes wounds to lick, desires unfulfilled and confusion about what is important. It is like the guy who got no sex from his marriage for 2 years so when he started looking for a relationship again all he could think about was getting sex; or the gal who had no intimacy in her marriage so her first more important thing in a new relationship at the moment is a sensitive guy who is focused on her even though she is attracted to bad boys. We all have these kinds of relationships. Most are failed experiments at trying to get what we missed.

What is normal anyway?

We define normal now-a-days as what about 80% of the people do. The 10% of each extreme end are abnormal. So for a relationship type to fall into the normal range it must be practiced by the 80% or some vast number within the 80%.

There are three types of relationships that fall as normal. The *Traditional male led relationship* MLR (though you may groan about the idea it is the most pervasive), the *transitional relationship* (what we do after break-ups – I also call this the healing relationship), and the *50/50 relationship*. All others fall outside the norm.

Because of the pervasive tradition men and women are both subject too, that even 50/50 relationships tend to bend towards being unequal. It is because of roles and gender. Consider household chores and protection as ideas. Because we are socialized this way it tends to fall on women to do more or all the housework and men grab the bat next to the bed to protect the family when we hear the window break.

So, inequality already exists in relationships for various and hard to define reasons. Sometimes the roles of men and women are "hopefully" defined based on our assumption that is how a "man is supposed to behave" or "that is women's work."

All this is leading up to how decisions are made, who controls the decision and what kinds of influences we can use as guiding principles.

Assumptions of our authority to make decisions by ourselves, and the expectations of the other member's agreement in joint decisions are bad presidents for couples. "If you loved me you'd!", she cried, "I naturally assumed" she said. "I expected more form you" he wounded.

Why is unequal important

Unequal is a sign to us all – a notice about human relationships and human nature. The sign is that despite our best rhetoric, intensions and values, we all still hold a relationship model that suits us as individuals and it might seem equal in some areas but weighed in the balance it is not, especially where couple decisions are concerned.

Further, we sometimes see ourselves as the better mate in our skills and abilities. Of course there are exceptions but the big paint brush approach to this picture is correct. This is our license to create change. It is our license to negotiate a better relationship. It is our license to be better mates. It is our license to become better people. We have a license to create a better relationship model and streamline decision making.

The myth and the legend

A myth is that relationships have to be like they are now. A myth is that people want 50/50 relationships. A myth is that people believe equality in a relationship is the best idea we have so far. Together these myths create the legend of the ideal relationship. Because we know how men and women feel about their counter parts in a relationship and their beliefs about their skills either we completely reprogram ourselves and our culture or we admit the ideal only works for ideal couples.

I want to believe in the ideal but I think it is a designer relationship that works for the two people in it not a broad brush approach to one size fits all.

Consider what women believe for a moment from one of our online surveys.

Who is better at communication?
Men 6% Women 85% Equal 10%

Who is better at leadership? (In relationships)
Men 11% Women 71% Equal 18%

Who is better at creating intimacy?
Men 4% Women 87% Equal 10%

I like the thought of leading a man?
Yes 73% In Some Ways 24% No 3%

I like the thought of managing our life?
Yes 72% In Some Ways 26% No 2%

I want him to be vulnerable to me?
Yes 78% On Cue 6% Sometimes 15% No 1%

So if these things are true and you can design a relationship to optimize areas of weakness, what would you design into your relationship?

Would you find a partner who was teachable who wanted to learn good communication or was already a good communicator? Would you take an active role in "leadership" in your relation because you expressed your belief that women are better at it than men? Would you manage your life as a couple because you are the better manager?

The possibilities are there and seeking likeminded people or working with our existing mates to become like minded gets us closer to the 'real ideal' that is ideal for us – and best of all it is not that much work because we all have to do those things anyway.

Summary: Relationships tend to be unequal even with the best intentions of those who want equal partners. Culture and strong human nature colors our view of "coupling up". It is better to openly discuss roles and authority to make decisions instead of the assumption of equality. This is our license to communicate, negotiate and seek better things. Relationships are unequal by our design.

You and your mate as whole "istic" people

Why do I need to know this?

People are complex and relationships make them more complex so visualizing people in relationships helps get to the root of fulfillment issues. This is the foundation for negotiation.

Relationship: two people + a thing

The comic said "*the trouble with relationships is there are two people in them*" and we all know wherever two are; there will be disagreements. Most people are not all that gifted as communicators so interpersonal relationships suffer. A second trouble people face is their willingness to take risks exposing themselves and their expectations, dreams and desires.

You and your mate = a relationship, so there are three things to consider: you as an individual, your mate as an individual and your relationship as a couple. Of course that equation changes further when we have offspring, there becomes a web of relationships.

Some women know this intuitively and express their understanding by saying "I'll do it for the sake of the relationship" recognizing that there is a thing she is connected to called 'relationship' and she is an individual too.

With decisions you might take any of three tactics in a relationship: for your benefit, for your mates benefit or for the benefit of the relationship. This elegantly sums up the nature of coupling up and the added complexity it gives to decisions.

2 People + the relationship have needs

Each member will have their own needs and desires. We learned in the information age that things such as relationships are part of life. We learned relationships can be experienced virtually as well as in the web like way families live. Relationship has a life of its own; it is the time it takes away from 'me' for 'we' time. There is a 'high importants' to it, a drive to "make it work". There are new rules, expectations, connections and desires at stake for the thing to fulfill the individuals in them.

Relationship got more complex

We experience life in more than one dynamic now, we are becoming more aware of people around us and more connected and that connection awareness has made us realize that needs of those things "such as relationships" we are connected to. The internet allows us to voyeuristically looking into the lives of others and experiments in ways we could not before. Before the information age we could only connect with those near us and now we can connect with thousands around the world to have relationship.

More examples of connected life beyond the individuals are the way we experience our careers. The modern career is sometimes so demanding it creates the necessity for our making our connecting with those we work with in exclusion of others because we just don't have time to keep relationships vital outside or work. Virtual relations take the place of keeping us connected to those we have little time for.

You are your mate and you both as a couple are not just you; you are a vast web of relationships both personal and virtual that play into your relationship dynamic as a couple. So considering the whole of you "all" is as important as considering the individual. Your contribution to the vast connected group you have will impact many and so your decisions as a couple and as individuals go.

Defining what we can change

The reason it is important to understand ourselves wholly is we behave differently depending on who we are with exposing elements of ourselves.

People are a bundle of three things.

1. **A core person** (something that changes little over time and best represents who you are.)
2. **An adaptive person** (things that we can change, negotiate and adapt too like how we

spend vacations or how we feel about politics or social causes; and how we handle decisions.)
3. **An extended person** (the us we are in our broader circle of relationships like the party animal you are with one friend and the quiet tea drinker you are with another)

Relationships are bundles of people who when interacting tend to define the relationship and us. When with a circle of women shopping you behave and project a different you then in other situations and that group responds to your projection.

Summary: Relationships and individuals are complex and thinking about it as whole "istic" improves our ability to see where we are in our ability to make decisions and negotiate.

*P*erspective on dating and new relationships

Why do I need to know this?

New relationships offer a perfect place to create a better cleaner more satisfying experience for both mates. Changing an existing relationship is harder.

Using the 5 food groups as a thought provoking primer to conversation?

I used the 5 food groups as a primer; to discuss how a woman felt about control and those areas we often have strife in relationships. They helped me go beyond personality to some of the more practical matters of relationship development. It is not something for small talk but once you get beyond the introduction phase it helps to ask questions since you both want to be in a relationship and want some assurance of longevity through compatibility.

By discussing the 5 food groups I understood the decision making model a woman desires and if she had thought about the issues couples face intelligently. By asking and listening to follow-up questions "what about this?" and "what about that?"

I was able to see how much control she desired, see some of her baggage left over from being burned in previous relationships and discern if she wanted an intelligent decision making model. In short it helped me refine my compatibility with her.

Why decision making is a better gauge for compatibility?

Personality, the laws of attraction and the "rules of engagement" are not very easy to develop science for but a person's track record of decision making reveals their core person to you. Consider what happens when you burn your hand on the stove, do you make different choices afterwards? Each time you near the stove do you remember what happened? So go all your decisions. People over 40 who couple up are more seasoned; they have burned their hands a few times in various ways and formed decision making patterns we can see by talking about common things we all engage in. It is the commonality of the 5 food groups that opens the way to discerning compatibility.

Why discussing control helps us live a life without drama and strife?

The desire for control is a response to our hierarchy of needs. If you had abandonment (security) issues, control looks good for those reasons. If you had a stability issue control looks good for that reason. Control further gets people to justify their reasons for their control revealing their guiding principles; even if they never could put voice to them before.

Real control is not really possible – yes I said not possible. In relationships that management/control requires willful participating from your mate. So toss out the idea control means a robot on the other end, it is more management, leadership and influence.

Why we have a license and a duty to "the relationship" to improve communication?

The silent partner you have in relationship is "the relationship" itself. It is definable so it exists. Since it has no voice we as its members must speak for it, improve it, help it grow. Voicing for the relationship is not work. It is an expression of love at seeing potential while looking at some area of relationship that does not work, then taking license to change it so it does.

There are a great many voices we listen to in our circle of friends and family. We listen to professionals, culture and somewhere are those voices we used to form our ideas about relationship.

No matter what voice you may have heard to the contrary. Whether you believe it or not; you are worthy to live a good life in a relationship that is fulfilling. Take license to enjoy creating intimacy, connection and companion ship that feels good.

*T*he big 2 food groups and control of all 5

Why do I need to know this?

Women we surveyed and interviewed resist the idea of control in relationships as a backlash to having felt controlled. The big 2 offer the best results with the least control.

The best of it for the least agreement?

An astute observer can see right off that *Finances* and *Free Time* have some properties that affect all the other food groups. For example to make the life decision to return to school you will need both time and money. By my calculation *Free Time* is the greater of the two because other than the time we work and the time it takes us to stay in good health all our time if free time, so in essence nothing can be done without it.

There are a lot of guys that are cropping up after they turn 40 years old or so who like the idea of females takes a more active role in leadership in a relationship. It seems many have become more open minded, see the benefits of two capable people instead of one, and have changed their overall view of women. Oddly women don't see this right off as an opportunity. To some it looks like something's amiss or it just looks like more work. The bottom line is there is room and license for both men and women to talk about control of the food groups.

Controlling the big two in a relationship may be ideal for any active growing couple with goals, who need a plan and some discipline to make it work. Like that retirement savings account that keeps slipping into the future or that dream of returning to finish your master's degree and moving up in management.

Controlling the big two has some real advantages in streamlining decision making and removing weakness and you can still have a democracy. Granting control over the big two just means there is now a governor who can keep you all on your path to the finish line.

Control of the big 2 or all 5 food groups means you can set a goals for yourself as a couple and have a cop there to say no, "we said we wanted to do this first, and this other things will distract us. " You can help each other by sharing the voice of reason.

The food groups give you the pattern you need to decide what is important and the control to be successful at it.

I read a blog talking about unequal relationship where a woman was leading a man and one woman said "I'll just stick with my 50/50 relationship". I thought about that and it seems so hollow that someone who is better at something could not share it in a relationship. Was she a lesser leader, with no skills that would benefit a relationship? Why would she shy away from sharing her leadership or any other talent? Why would a man? A relationship where she was a benefit to him and he to her just by being themselves sound better - right?

*U*nderstanding the dynamics of decision making

Why do I need to know this?

This section will make you smarter in the way you approach decisions and in designing governance in your relationship that is optimized for both mates and the relationship.

Decisions Decisions

The word decision is another word for choice. Decision making is part of all we do as people. We decide to get out of bed in the morning and what to wear to work or play. Decision making is much simpler when it effects and requires just one person. The dynamic of decision making changes when we get two people making decisions. The interaction between two deciders creates an opportunity for positive feedback or tension.

Decision Making Models

Fact based decision making is a method for making a decision after gathering facts and weighting them then choosing accordingly. Fact based decisions sometimes leave out matters of the heart and feelings.

There are some who favor the "quick decision" or "I'll follow my guy" decision in relationships *Emotion based decision making* sometimes does not take into account the impact of a decision sacrificing the future for the moment.

Those in business and science use decision making models such as "balanced score card" or "quantitative analysis", "rational decision making models" and so on. These models provide defined steps to come to a conclusion but may not cover all aspects of the effects decisions have.

Decision Making Weights

Besides the decision making models there are different weights to decisions. Choosing blue or brown pants does not carry the same weight to consequence most often as choosing a $60,000 car. Similarly choosing not to go out on a date and choosing to get a divorce have a much different weight.

Decisions for three

There is a strange dynamic in relationships, a silent third party named "the relationship" that is often the reason for beneficiary of decisions. "I'll do it for the sake of the relationship" is one of those statements that acknowledge the existing of the union of the couple, the place where the individuals intersect.

In relationships there are some decisions a couple may never share. A couple my never share grooming decision or health choices. They may never share choices about separate assets.

Decision Best Practice

The best practice in relationships is to adopt a hybrid decision making model appropriate to the weight of the decision's impact on the individuals and the relationship. Consider a situation where a mate gets a job offer in another state which is really good but the other mate does not want to move for any number of reasons. You can see how that kind of decision making cannot be strictly rational, fact based or emotional because the consequence of a bad decision is daunting.

Decision Making Models for Unequal Relationships

When a mate has decision making control over a food group they may include the other mate in the decision making process or not depending on their agreement. Suppose a mate has control over household chores by agreement of the couple. That mate chooses a high standard and a certain decor. To change a sofa there may be no need for discussion and no impact on the mate or the relationship. But in the case where the other mate must change their lifestyle because of the choice of the mate in control discussion is both wise and warranted.

Decision making in unequal relationships often does not include the other mate; that is why it is desirable and more efficient. Having a skillful manager bound by limits is an optimized decision model. Making agreements in advance with limitations makes day to day management easier.

*U*nderstanding authority, control & responsibility

Why do I need to know this?

This section is a primer to solving personal objections and your mate's objections to certain words which often get knee jerk reactions.

What is control?

Control is just another word for manage and manage is another word for leadership. Everyone has to manage their affairs. We manage our finances, our social calendar and our life direction as surely as we breathe and sleep. Controlling a thing does not mean you actually do it, you might have someone else do it and you just manage the actual decisions as they occur.

There are three kinds of control: shared control, functional control and ultimate control.

Shared control works somewhere near 50/50 where both partners agree to make decision together but one partner may have some added responsibility but not authority to exceed that they both agreed upon: such as who writes the checks.

Functional control is best expressed as lacking "ultimate control and looks like level of 1/99 – 99/1 until a final decision or veto is needed. One member may use the finances more than another such as in a family business but not have the permission of their mate to bind the couple to long term financial agreements without permission. Functional control means "within limits"

Ultimate control means you can either veto or decide independently with or without your mate's permission. This looks like 100/0-0/100.

Authority is another word for permission to decide. In the case of shared control one mate brings the issue to a decision point then the both vote. In the case of functional control the mate has permission to a certain level and in ultimate control the mate no longer needs permission, they are empowered to proceed.

Responsibility is word for who is accountable for executing duties and tasks. In no way does having responsibility imply authority. The two are mutually exclusive. Think about one mate paying the bills and using the joint checking account to do so, that does not also give them the authority to invest in stocks, save money, or use the money for any other purpose. This is important because people make assumptions of authority which often caused issues of trust later.

I have heard people say "I don't want to control anyone or anything in my relationship alone", I think assuming a 50/50 relationship affords them the freedom of shared decision control. What they have done by saying that is set a pit full of sharp spiked ends as a trap for themselves when it comes to decision making control.

The underlying reason people grow distant is because they are not getting their needs met in a relationship.

What women seem to want to control

Many relationships have a role in them that "pays the bills". This simple role might not have the authority to make financial decisions beyond "the bills".

In a survey we took at one of our websites we surveyed women and asked "Why controls the finances" to which 50% or so said the woman did. But she did not have "final say" in spending. Most couples worked that out together and only 60% of women said they wanted the final say in finances.

Women, in our survey, expressed an interest in control over all 5 good groups and some other areas of behavior of men.

I want to control Finances
Yes 50% Final Word 24% Shared 22% No 5%

I want to control his Free Time
Yes 46% Final Word 32% Shared 19% No 2%

I want to control Sex
Yes 59% Final Word 26% Shared 11% No 4%

I want to control our Life Direction
Yes 42% Final Word 39% Shared 19% No 1%

I want to control Household Chores
Yes 70% Final Word 16% Shared 14% No 1%

In our survey women expressed interest in control at some level and when it was already in their assumed control space that interest rose dramatically.

Women in our surveys were also interested in behavior. These high interests are points for negotiation.

I want him to seek my advice?
Yes 78% Depends 22% No 0%

I want him to seek my approval?
Yes 83% Depends 17% No 0%

I want him to make himself attractive for me?
Yes 93% Depends 6% No 1%

I want him to ask me what help he can be?
Yes 100% Depends 0% No 0%

I want him to appreciate me openly?
Yes 96% Depends 4% No 0%

I want him to keep a nice home?
Yes 95% Depends 4% No 1%

I want him to comfort me?
Yes 85% On Cue 11% No 4%

I want him to desire to spend time with me?
Yes 91% Depends 9% No 0%

I want him to desire me sexually?
Yes 88% On Cue 11% No 1%

I heard many times women say "why don't men just do these things without having to get something in return?" and to some extent they do, it is to the extent the woman desires that is deficient and having control of the food groups gives women more power to negotiate the finer points of behavior which men can easily change and likely want to once they are alerted to their woman's desire.

Why would a man give up control?

Men want things to and they may want behavioral changes in you. They may also trust a woman's skills as being better than their in some areas. There is also a segment of men who want female led relationships where women have more control then men. Since you are in a relationship and the goal of a couple is to be fulfilled by the association men tend to favor trading for fulfillment. Think of it like a designer relationship, where it becomes custom crafted just for you.

The closer you were in your compatibility when you started the closer you will be to fulfillment through negotiation.

Why woman want to take control?

At a base level control looks like it also has security inherent in it and it has been suggested that is why women want it. But because his willful participation is required to get control and he can revoke that; the security is somewhat of an illusion.

Couples get into operational entanglement after sometime by sharing things and depending on each other for things. Control simply streamlines decision making in a relationship.

Good management and decision making skills applied to a relationship reduces strife and creates a platform for trust and fulfillment of those higher desires mates have. Since my mother's time most women have worked, colleges are filled with women educating themselves in business and arts, teaching and nursing. We are in the information age but also in the age of the professional woman. These great dynamic means women are feeling better about leadership, control and getting smarter about relationship dynamics.

The best reason to control of to build a better relationship where everyone gets what they want.

Charting your course as a couple

The best, fastest, and more useful decision making between couples happens when some ground work is laid. Have a conversation or a series of conversations to get through the list below. You will be making discoveries about you, your mate and your relationship.

1. Talk openly about the food groups, how you make decisions.
    a. Discuss what if's and situations you have experienced that were trouble.
    b. Explore your hard boundaries by discussing situational ethics and choices. "What would you do if?", "how would you handle?"
2. Select a temporary manager (a placeholder) for each food group based on interest.
    a. This will be an area of influence but not a license control.
    b. If you cannot agree on a manager no worries, choose shared control with one person managing the food group so you don't need management by committee.
3. Discuss your expectations about each food group.
    a. Consider your hierarchy of needs here, your must haves and your like to haves.

       b. Consider situations and desires you want. You can make trades for things you want and your mate is willing to trade with.

       c. This is a good chance to be transparent

4. Set any limits and grant authority to make decisions to the manager

       a. This is your license and authority so you don't need to wonder anymore.

5. Discuss how you want communication from the manager about what they are doing or about to do.

6. Set a time limit to your agreement and don't jump ship at the first incident, talk it out casually as needed and support the decisions of your mate.

7. Arrange a regular date meeting for casual conversation and adjustments to your agreement.

8. Record your conversation as notes or in an agreement or digitally so you can refer to it in the future.

Your discussions will empower you and your mate to have less strife, better communication and faster better decision making. You'll know each other better and have connected at a level most couples can't rise too.

Creating intimacy and communication with the food groups

This is a short chapter on what you can achieve because of the 5 food groups and someone managing them. Couples wanting to grow in their fulfillment can use control of the food groups to guide their partners. Suppose a woman desires more intimacy in sex and beyond it, she can either control sex as a management function or she can negotiate with her mate to get the improvements she desires it is just that simple.

Many men through their social training learn to compartmentalize. Compartmentalization is was way of dealing with all kinds of emotional situations. The compartmentalized man has real difficulty being intimate or connected. Men are discovering they are missing some connections that are meaningful and expressing their desire for connection and intimacy.

This is one example many men and women look forward to in the 30's and 40's after years of unmet desire the possibility of fulfillment become more real because a) you can discuss it openly and b) there is a management function for it created by the 5 food groups.

Fulfillment is what makes relationships satisfying. Couple can jump to the top of the pyramid but it is more advisable for a sustainable fulfillment that each member fulfills the precursors to intimacy first then work your way up the pyramid until you get there. Life will become more fulfilling in many ways by following the pyramid upward and it will be an adventure.

I recommend discussing it. Some men get lazy about connection and intimacy because of the experiences they had and the fact is it is easier to do less and be disconnected. You may open his eyes OR you may just be preaching to the choir.

Here is a proposed path:

Basic Connection: I am connected to another person in a relationship where we both are committed to each other.

Relationship Stability: Before trying anything new stabilize your relationship. This is a safety issue so mates can extend more trust. If you have arguments and one person withdraws or a mate has fear of relationship failure all the activities beyond will be tainted and stressful. This does not mean you don't have stress, it just means you know your mate will be there for you tomorrow.

Intimacy: begin practicing those things that create and sustain intimacy including sex. Vulnerability, share expectations, time in private together, massage, gestures of love.

Confidence and re-aligned images: Begin to see your mate as your partner in fulfillment, capable and trustworthy. Grow your confidence in intimacy, leadership and the stability of your relationship. Give a little trust and help your mate keep it. Never set up anyone to fail, set them up to succeed. Learn from mistakes, benefit from criticisms, and brainstorm solutions.

Anywhere you want to go from there is up to you.

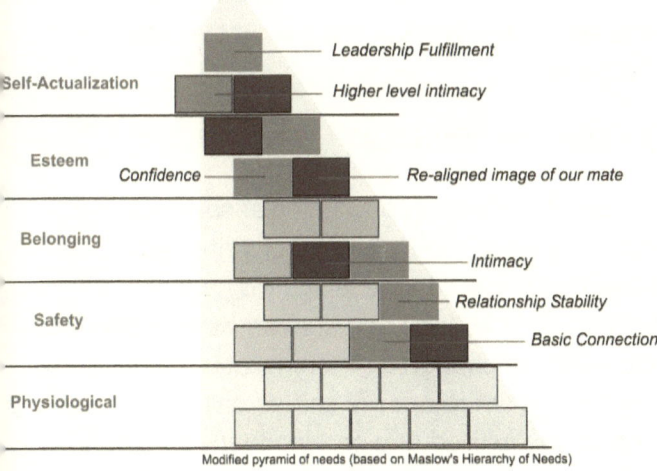

Modified pyramid of needs (based on Maslow's Hierarchy of Needs)

Tempted to jump to the good stuff? Many people concentrate on the goodies but find out that they are unsustainable and not all that fulfilling because "something is missing." The missing things are the building blocks for sustainability.

Understanding the hierarchy of human needs in relationships

Why do I need to know this?

This section will help you visualize the path to wonderful fulfillment in your relationship for both you and your mate by visualizing what the steps are to get there.

Needs and desires

Maslow the Russian psychologist summed up the human experience by a hierarchy of needs. The base needs were those things we cannot live without such as food and shelter, as the tiers rise those needs change to less critical more desirable needs until at the apex is self-actualization" meaning one is fully fulfilled and sharing that with others.

Each member in your relationship has needs and desires and those may be quite different. For instance: women may deeply desire an intimate experience while men want an external one and the couple desires connection (a sense of belonging). Each member gets to self-actualization by a different path because the members fulfill their desires at their own pace and in their own way.

One example for a couple is "coupling up". Each member has a reason to couple up and the relationship needed definition after sometime so there was a sense of connection. Coupling up may solve basic needs for food and shelter and higher needs for connection and intimacy.

Basic needs for a relationship

Relationships and the individuals in them solve some problems by creating several more. Relationships beyond procreation seek to solve the basic human needs for connection, belonging and security. While adding the problems of decision making, possible strife and well…. you can list this yourself.

When you entered into a relationship you literally traded something for what you are getting. You know, you give something to your mate and to the relationship and get something in return from your mate and from the relationship. A good trade all in all.

In relationships there are higher ideals beyond the basic needs met by coupling up. Women often hope for intimacy, greater connection, support from her mate, and a good sex life. You all know relationships that have none of these and they are still together. So as long as the baser needs are met many couples stay together and don't seek the higher ideals. What is "good enough" to stay in a relationship is up to those in it.

The higher needs become obvious when our baser needs are met, so when he get some semblance of connection, we then begin to see we have been missing intimacy or greater connection and any number of higher needs.

Higher needs for a relationship

Defining your desires helps you see where you can go; defining where you are helps you see the difference. Let's say a woman want to experience ultimate intimacy in her relationship. She wants Tantra sex with her mate to experience the trills of surrender. To get it you must first experience some lover level desires like intimacy and higher connection so she has some work and needs a willing mate to get her closer to fulfillment.

It is like learning to crawl before you walk and then run. There is a path, there is fulfillment available but there is also some steps that need to be taken before you get there.

Food groups to the rescue

In a 50/50 relationship the woman would need to negotiate with her mate and may or may not be successful. If the woman has control of some or all of the couple's free time or sex then she can make it happen

Understanding negotiation dynamics

To have a successful negotiation both parties in the event must win. Compromise means both parties lose something or one loses everything and while that may pass as a completed agreement it is not very satisfying for either party.

The best negotiation result is when both parties get what they want or are willing to trade for something else that they want. This is possible much of the time when each mate as a basket of goodies they are willing to trade.

People ascribe various weights to things they own. Some of the things you own are precious to you and something's are not. One thing I learned in life is I can do things I don't like for a short time but after a while it drives me nuts, so when trading, inside your goodie basket will be all kinds of things and many of them will be enjoyable to trade, but some will be odious and difficult to sustain. I recommend you trade things you really like for things your mate does so the experience is positive for you both and your relationship benefits or set a time limit.

When trading something you don't like to do very much consider its weight, so you get something much better in return.

Overcoming objections

There are reasons that men and women may not want to participate in the food group negotiations and discussions. Most of them can be overcome by discussing situational examples. This book has been about the reasons you should discuss them.

Organic discussions happen when the ideas presented are associated during some event related to the ideas. In other words you don't discuss mathematics at the ballet nor do you discuss tonight's dinner during love making, they just don't mesh together well.

The reaction to the food groups for most open minded people will be one of interest. You both may decide to modify the ideas in this book to fit your relationship and situation; but what to do about objections?

Remember you are not selling anything; this is about choosing a method of management to cover the basic decisions all couple make routinely as part of relationship. Everyone will agree that things must be managed to some extent, so the form of management is all you are addressing.

People generally want to trust and believe in their mates. If you don't enjoy trust in your relationship you have much bigger things to fix before you can address decision making.

"*I like things as they are*" – Ask questions about their satisfaction level with each of the 5 food groups. Discuss your level of satisfaction.

"*It looks too complicated*" – Ask them to suggest a simpler way. Discuss how decisions are made now and if it is effective.

"*I always thought I was in charge of that*" – Discuss how that expectation got started and what is reinforcing it.

"*How do I know this will work?*" – It works every day between couples around the world; this is just a formal acknowledgement of how it works.

"*How do we know who is better at something?*" – The premise is the mate managing is not doing it in a vacuum, you can continue to discuss things and the mate managing can learn to become more decisive and to make better choices.

"*What exactly are we trading*?" – You are trading unspoken unmet expectations, poor communication, no path to fulfillment – FOR -- more formal management for greater fulfillment, increased communication growing in trust and advanced connection; trade free time for better sex, trade control for benefits; trade stress for harmony.

Learn to discuss things not people. If you keep your discussion to things you'll have less chance of hurting someone you love.

Where to get help

www.5-food-groups.com has a place to ask questions and share experiences. We are in the information age, take advantage of all the information people are willing to share.

Help Me with Relationships Series

Author M. Lyman Hill is creating a series of books to help women and men with their relationships and internet dating experiences.

- **Why Do I Keep Picking The Wrong Guy?**
  - Internet dating help for women who pick the wrong men over and over again. First in this series.
- **How Can I Attract The Right Guy For Me?**
  - More Internet dating help for women who pick the wrong men over and over again. Second in this series.
- **How Can I Attract The Right Guy For Me?**
  - Internet dating help for women who pick the wrong men over and over again. The final books in this series of three.
- **Help Me Find My Soul Mate**
  - Internet dating help for women and men in finding what really matters in relationships.
- **The 5 Food Groups** - Negotiating In Relationships
  - Relationship help for couples and those looking for better relationships.
- **Help Me Find A Relationship Model That Works For Me**
  - A fresh perspective on what makes good relationships in the information age.
- **Help Me Save My Relationship**
  - A quick help guide for women who want to save their relationship.
- **Why Men Become Lazy Lovers** (what to do about it)
  - Relationship help for women

Help Me Find My
SoulMate

Internet dating help for women and men in
finding what really matters in relationships

One hour of your
time reading
this book will
enlighten you

By M. Lyman Hill

author of My First 32 Coffee Dates

Available spring 2011

www.ingramcontent.com/pod-product-compliance
Lightning Source LLC
Chambersburg PA
CBHW031329290526
45784CB00014B/2456